RACING MANIA

DRAG RACING

K.C. KELLEY

This edition first published in 2010 in the United States
of America by Marshall Cavendish Benchmark.

Marshall Cavendish Benchmark
99 White Plains Road
Tarrytown, NY 10591-5502
www.marshallcavendish.us

Library of Congress Cataloging-in-Publication Data
Kelley, K. C.
Drag Racing / by K. C. Kelley.
p. cm. — (Racing mania)
Summary: "Provides comprehensive information on the history, the famous faces, the design,
and the performance of the amazing machines behind Drag Racing"—Provided by publisher.
Includes bibliographical references and index.
ISBN 978-0-7614-4384-1
Includes bibliographical references and index.
1. Drag racing—Juvenile literature. I. Title.
GV1029.3.K44 2009
796.72—dc22
2009004532

Cover: shutterstock
Half Title: Auto Imagery Inc.
pp4-5: Auto Imagery Inc.; p5: Shutterstock; pp6-7: Hulton Archive/Getty Images;
p7: National Geographic/Getty Images; pp8-9: Auto Imagery Inc.; p9: Auto Imagery Inc.;
pp10-11: Auto Imagery Inc.; p11: Auto Imagery Inc.; p12: Auto Imagery Inc.; p13: Auto Imagery Inc.;
pp14_15; p16: Auto Imagery Inc.; p17: Auto Imagery Inc.; p18-19: Auto Imagery Inc.;
p19: Auto Imagery Inc.; p20: Auto Imagery Inc.; p21: Auto Imagery Inc.; p22-23: Auto Imagery Inc.;
p23: Auto Imagery Inc.; p24: Auto Imagery Inc.; p25: Auto Imagery Inc.; pp26-27: Auto Imagery Inc.;
p27: Auto Imagery Inc.; p28: Auto Imagery Inc.; p29: Auto Imagery Inc.; pp30-31: Auto Imagery Inc.;
p32: Auto Imagery Inc.; p33: Auto Imagery Inc.; p34: Auto Imagery Inc.; p35: Auto Imagery Inc.; p36:
Auto Imagery Inc.; p37: Auto Imagery Inc.; p38: Rusty Jarrett/Getty Images;
p39: Ronald C. Modra/Sports Imagery/Getty Images; p40: Auto Imagery Inc.;
p41: Auto Imagery Inc.; p42: Auto Imagery Inc.; p43: Auto Imagery Inc.

Created by Q2AMedia
Editor: Denise Pangia
Series Editor: Jim Buckley
Art Director: Sumit Charles
Client Servicing Manager: Santosh Vasudevan
Project Manager: Shekhar Kapur
Designer: Joita Das and Shilpi Sarkar
Photo Research: Shreya Sharma

Printed in Malaysia

1 3 5 6 4 2

CONTENTS

INTRODUCTION

In drag racing, it's all about speed.

All motor sports are about going faster than the other vehicles. One type of motor sport is the fastest race around: drag racing. Drag racing is simple. Two cars race side by side on a short, quarter-mile (0.4 kilometer) track. The first car to reach the finish line wins. Races take just a few seconds. The racing cars reach speeds above 300 miles per hour (480 km/hour)! But the amount of training, work, and technology that go into those several seconds is enormous.

One of the popular types of dragsters are Funny Cars. This car is not on fire. The smoke comes from the fast-spinning tires just before the start of a race.

Drag racing has unique cars and ways of racing. It's very different from NASCAR (National Association for Stock Car Auto Racing) or Formula 1. In drag racing, the tracks are just about 400 yards (120 meters) long, so fans can see every second of the racing action.

How fast are dragsters? The best cars can go as fast as a rocket leaving a launch pad. A super-fast Porsche Turbo passenger car goes from 0 to 100 miles per hour (0 to 161 km/h) in about 10 seconds. It takes a Top Fuel dragster 0.8 seconds to reach the same speed.

Strap on your helmet, clear the track, and watch the Christmas Tree (What's that? Stay tuned!). You're about to go drag racing!

Porsches are among the fastest cars you see on the street. Their powerful engines are no match for those used in drag racing.

■ INSIDE STORY ||||||

The Basic Cars

There are three basic types of vehicles used in drag racing:

Top Fuel: Long, thin, and lightweight—these odd-looking cars are the fastest dragsters. Their enormous rear wheels contrast with their tiny front wheels.

Funny Car: Based on real-life car models, but with wild designs and exaggerated body types, these cars are so fast, it's not funny!

Pro Stock: These are racing cars modified with much more powerful engines.

EARLY DRAGSTERS

Ever since the second car was made, so the saying goes, people have been racing.

From the earliest days of the automobile age, racing has played a big part in sports. NASCAR (National Association for Stock Car Auto Racing) gets a lot of attention these days. Its races pack giant tracks with fans and draw millions of TV viewers. Around the world, Formula 1 has turned its drivers into international superstars. But, drag racing is the motor sport most widely practiced in the United States.

In a drag race, two cars are placed side by side on a quarter-mile (0.4 km) track. From a standing start, they roar away, trying to be first and fastest. This high-energy style of racing has been popular since the 1920s. Some owners of Ford Model Ts and Model As figured out how to tinker with the engine to make their cars go faster.

Southern California was—and remains—America's hotbed of drag racing. Those first drag racers sped on hard and flat dry lake beds is northeast of Los Angeles. They were known as hot rodders. Accidents were not uncommon. Many injuries and deaths resulted. But the racers kept going.

The Creation. In 1932 the Ford V-8 engine kicked drag racing into a new gear. It had twice as much power as older four-cylinder engines. By the late 1930s, so many people were taking part in this fast-growing (and fast-moving) sport that many organizations sprang up to help them race safely. A sport that was once considered an outlaw was becoming respectable!

■ INSIDE STORY ▐▐▐▐▐▐

Why Lake Beds?

To have a great drag race, you need a space that's long, flat, and level. Even city streets are not perfect, as they might have bumps or curves. Drag racers found the perfect solution in the lake beds of Lake Muroc, among others, northeast of Los Angeles. Airplane runways were another popular spot. Farther east, vast areas of salt flats, actually oceans long ago, now as flat as a sheet of paper for miles around, provided perfect raceways. In fact, the Bonneville Salt Flats near Bakersfield remains the best place in the world for attempts to break all sorts of land speed records.

This dragster from a 1963 race looks different from today's racers. These early cars were made of steel and aluminum and had larger front tires. But they were still very, very fast!

SETTLING DOWN

Drag racing really took off after World War II, as the need for speed among veterans met a new spirit of an organization.

World War II, which the United States entered after the attack of Pearl Harbor by the Japanese on December 7, 1941, stopped most drag racing. When the soldiers and sailors returned from the war, many of them got involved in drag racing and car making. They had enjoyed the speed of airplanes and other military vehicles, and had tested their courage in combat. Because of the war, many advances were made in engineering and **aerodynamics**. Passenger cars became longer, sleeker, and faster. Drag racers did the same—but focused on the faster part!

In 1946 a group of veterans started the Southern California Timing Association (SCTA). Drag racing depends a lot on accurate timing, so the association worked to standardize the timing and safety issues among racers. Drivers and race organizers worked together to arrange better, safer races. They also developed systems to ensure that racers competed against cars of similar speed and power. They held speed weeks, during which dozens of races were held every day, and later helped open the Santa Ana Drags, one of the first official drag strips.

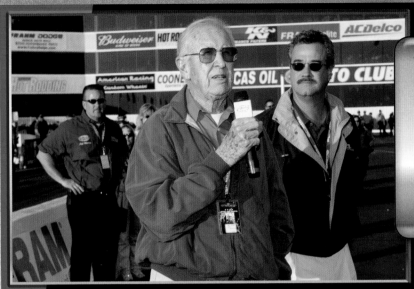

Wally Parks (holding microphone) played a huge part in the growth of drag racing. He formed the first national organization. He called for more safety for drivers. He also helped promote the sport to more and more fans.

At the heart of all this was Wally Parks, the first head of SCTA. His leadership was a big part of drag racing's early success. Parks and others knew that to expand the sport, they'd need even more planning.

In 1951, after becoming the editor of *Hot Rod* magazine, Parks helped start the National Hot Rod Association (NHRA), and became its first president. Drag racing had really joined the big time.

Handmade hot rods like these were often seen at drag races. Drivers added parts to make their cars as fast as possible.

■ INSIDE STORY ▐▐▐▐▐▐

Robert Petersen

Along with Parks, another key figure in drag racing's early development was Robert Petersen. He started publishing *Hot Rod* magazine in 1948 and later became publisher of dozens of important automotive magazines, including *Motor Trend* and *Motorcyclist*. His support of motor sports through magazines, events, and publicity helped move drag racing from outsider's status into the mainstream. Though Petersen died in 2007, his legacy and his magazines—along with an amazing automobile museum in Los Angeles—live on every time a drag racer hits the strip.

THE NHRA

Drag racing started out as an outlaw sport, but today, it runs like a business.

Since its founding in 1951, the NHRA has grown into one of the largest motor sport organizations in the world. More than 35,000 drivers take part in its races on at least 140 tracks.

Fans pack the stands at both sides of this drag race track in Denver, Colorado. The workers on the track will move before the race starts.

The winners of different racing classes gather on the podium after a day's racing program is over. Trophies for everyone!

The NHRA held its first major event in 1953. By 1955 it was holding a national championship event at a different track each year. Other events were added over the years as more and more drivers wanted to show off their need for speed.

As cars got faster, the NHRA kept up. New car classes and types of fuel were added. All throughout, the NHRA worked to make its races fair, safe, and exciting.

Today's NHRA is best known for its three main classes of racing: Top Fuel, Funny Car, and Pro Stock. NHRA also runs classes of racing at lower levels, as well as amateur events. In addition, the NHRA runs Pro Stock Motorcycle drag races.

You are about to take a trip to a drag race and find out how these amazing machines are made. So put your pedal to the metal, and let's go!

TOP FUEL CARS

When most people think of drag racing, they think of Top Fuel cars.

Among dragsters, Top Fuel cars generally differ most from the cars people drive. A massive engine powers the cars' long, thin bodies. The engine is powerful enough to take the car from a standing start to 340 miles per hour (550 km/h) in just over 4 seconds. How fast is that? A Top Fuel car can drive the length of a football field in 1 second! If it could maintain top speed, a Top Fuel car could circle your school's track in just 4 seconds!

Top Fuel dragsters look different from any other motor vehicle. The driver sits in a tiny cockpit at the rear of the car. In front of him or her is a long, thin body made of very lightweight material. The body can be as long as 25 feet (8 m)! The massive engine is at the rear of the car. There is also a wing as wide as the car behind the driver. As air flows over this wing, it pushes the car down on the track and helps keep the car from flipping over.

Parachute

Top Wing

Engine

Cockpit

Front wing

A large parachute pops out of the back of the Top Fuel dragster to help it slow down from top speed.

Flames shooting out? Don't worry. The driver is just burning off a little fuel before starting the race.

Top Fuel dragsters have enormous rear wheels, more than 4 feet (1.2 m) tall. They are also very wide to give the car more **traction**, or grip, on the racing surface. To increase that grip, drivers do a burnout just before the race. The means spinning the wheels very fast, but not moving too far. The spinning heats up the tires and makes the rubber sticky. This stickiness helps the tires get the grip they need when that powerful engine kicks in.

The cars have tiny front wheels. Since drivers are just going in a straight line, they don't need much steering. The tiny wheels keep the weight of the vehicle down and allow the driver to steer the car straight.

▌ INSIDE STORY ▐▌▐▌▐▌

The Fuel

While the body of the Top Fuel dragster is unique, it's the fuel that runs the engine that gives the class its name. Top Fuel cars run on a mixture of two very powerful chemicals: **nitromethane** (90 percent) and **methanol** (10 percent). Both are basically explosives! They give the engine about three times as much power as regular gasoline used in other racing machines. Nitromethane can't be used in the engines of cars most people drive, and certainly can't carry a car very far. But it sure can make that car move fast! (The fuel used in Top Fuel dragsters costs nearly $20 per gallon!)

FUNNY CARS

These cars are so fast, it's not funny!

What's so funny about the high-speed brutes called Funny Cars? The name comes from when they were first made. Car makers moved the front wheels on standard cars forward to help balance the cars better at high speeds. They also began to make single-piece fiberglass bodies designed to slip through the air. And they placed all that on a frame, or chassis, made of steel tubing. The result looked like a car, but a funny one, with an odd shape, or a slightly **irregular** form. No one knows who made the first Funny Car, but whoever came up with it, people liked it, and it meant that Funny Cars were here to stay.

Funny Cars were a big part of drag racing in the 1960s and 1970s. In fact, until the Top Fuel dragsters came along in the 1970s, Funny Cars were at the top of the drag racing popularity scale. Among the heroes of those days were Gene Snow, Randall Liberman, and Don Garlits. By 1974 the NHRA was holding an annual Funny Car championship. It created a strict set of rules to make the competition fair. These rules included the size and type of engine, the spacing of the wheels, the weight of the car, and the operation of the engine itself.

Driver John Force has achieved the most wins in NHRA history and starred in *Funny Cars*, a TV series about his racing family. He's one of the all-time best in all motor sports.

The powerful engines used in Funny Cars spew out super-hot exhaust. The metal pipes on the side of the car release the hot gases from the engine. They can sometimes shoot out as flames, too.

Today, Funny Cars run on the same fuel used by Top Fuel cars and also use similar engines. Their wider shape and smaller wheels mean they can't quite reach the same high speeds as Top Fuel cars—but they come close! The best Funny Car drivers, such as the legendary John Force, can reach more than 300 miles per hour (500 km/h). The bodies of Funny Cars are made of carbon fiber, a type of material that is very strong and yet lightweight.

▮INSIDE STORY ▮▮▮▮▮▮

Beep, Beep Jeeps!

Drivers and car fans used just about every kind of car shape and body as the starting point for Funny Cars in the 1960s and 1970s. Dodge Darts, Ford Broncos, Pontiac GTOs, and Chevrolet Corvettes were often souped-up and ready to race. And some creative types took Jeeps and turned them into really odd-looking Funny Cars, perhaps with an eye for their military past. With the square fronts and long wheelbase, Funny Cars really stood out. Some drivers did have some success with them, though today's Funny Car races are all Jeep-free!

PRO STOCK CARS

Compared to other dragsters, Pro Stock cars are slow. But they would still blow you off the road!

Pro Stock cars are most similar to the cars we drive. That is, the designs are similar to the ones you might see in your family garage or out on the street. But, the resemblance stops at the body shape. Under the hood, these cars boast 500 cubic-inch (8,194 cubic-centimeter) engines that can put out more than 1,300 **horsepower** (your average family sedan does about 200 hp). These powerful engines rocket the car down the strip in excess of 200 miles per hour (320 km/h).

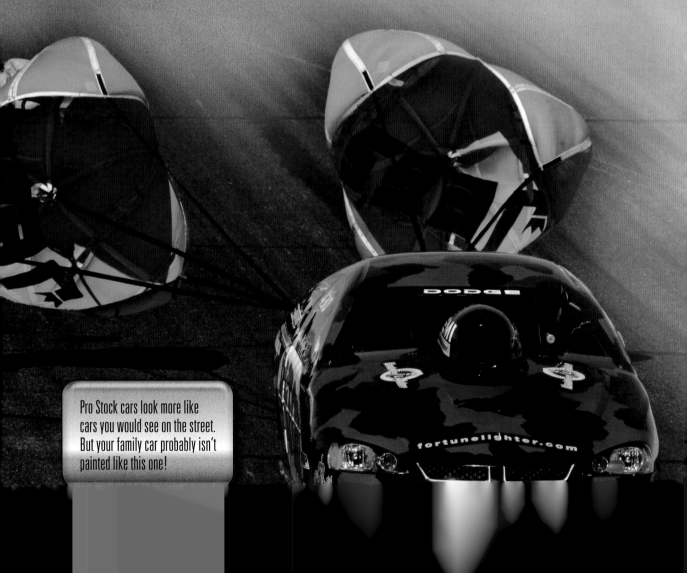

Pro Stock cars look more like cars you would see on the street. But your family car probably isn't painted like this one!

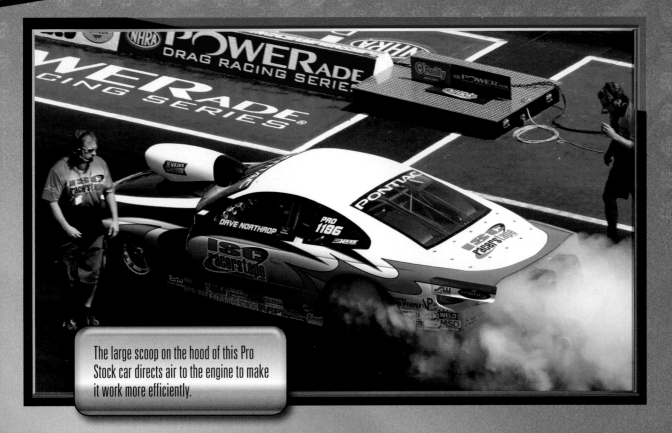

The large scoop on the hood of this Pro Stock car directs air to the engine to make it work more efficiently.

A big difference between Pro Stock and other NHRA classes is the fuel. Top Fuel and Funny Cars use a nitromethane mix. Pro Stock cars use gasoline and are also heavier, partly because of their steel-tube skeleton. In a race, a Pro Stock car and the driver weigh at least a combined 2,350 pounds (1,068 kilograms). That's more than 100 pounds (45.5 kg) more than a Top Fuel car. In a sport where the difference between winning and losing can be thousandths of a second, that weight becomes important.

Pro Stock got its biggest boost in the early 1970s. While the sport had been equally open to pros and amateurs, by the 1970s automakers began to put more money behind drivers. They wanted to showcase their cars for consumers. Sponsoring drivers and cars was a great way to do that. Since Pro Stock cars were more like the cars most people drove, this type of racing was most affected by this new source of money.

■ INSIDE STORY ▐▐▐▐▐▐

From Street to Track

The cars that are used in today's Pro Stock races are similar to what you might see on the street. All of the models must be from 2003 or later. The most popular types raced in recent years include Dodge Stratus, Pontiac GTO, Chevrolet Cobalt, and Pontiac G6 GXP. Their engines are made by the same companies, but they are put together differently than those sold to the drivers of the cars you see on the street today. The Pro Stock guys want a lot more power!

PRO STOCK MOTORCYCLES

High speed on two wheels—another way to drag race.

Even motorcycles look fast, don't they? Whipping past you on the highway or zooming around the track, bikes are built for speed. Drag racers have their own speedy bikes—Pro Stock Motorcycles, another NHRA racing class.

The NHRA has crowned a national champion in motorcycle drag racing every year since 1987. The motorcycles are built according to a long list of rules laid down by NHRA, but all the bikes can top 190 miles per hour (305 km/h). They fly through a quarter-mile (0.4 km) in less than 7 seconds, smoke flying from their burning tires! In fact, Angelle Sampey

The long, thin device at the back of the drag motorcycle helps the driver keep it from flipping backward due to the high speed.

At the start of the race, the powerful engines actually force the front wheel of the drag motorcycle off of the ground.

set a record for **elapsed time** in 2007 at 6.871 seconds. (In 2000 Angelle Sampey became the second woman ever to win a national motor sports title—joining Top Fuel's Shirley Muldowney—and Sampey won again in 2001 and 2002.)

Suzuki, a Japanese company, made most of the winning bikes in Pro Stock until 2003, when Harley-Davidson, a U.S. company, decided to challenge them. Today many fans watch the competition between these two huge companies as much as they watch the riders who steer the bikes on the track. Motorcycle racing may not get as much attention as the cars in drag racing, but these high-tech bikes and brave riders also deserve cheers!

■ INSIDE STORY |||||||

Motorcycle Stars

Dave Schultz was the first **dominant** motorcycle drag star. He won six NHRA titles from 1987–1996. The Hines family has a crowded mantelpiece. Brothers Matt (1997–1999) and Andrew Hines (2004–2006) have each won three national championships. Andrew would have won a fourth, but Matt Smith squeezed him out by just six points in the final race of 2007. Matt kept on rolling, taking the 2008 title as well.

A DRAG RACE

You just learned about the cars, now let's find out how they race.

In most motor sports, the cars are actually moving when the race begins. Drag racing is quite different. The two cars start side by side at one end of the quarter-mile (0.4 km) track. Cars match up for a race at most drag racing events. One wins and one loses. The winner continues on to race others; the losers are done for the day!

The most important thing on the track for the drag racers, other than their cars, is the Christmas Tree. This is the tall, metal pole standing between the two race cars. It has two rows of lights. The drivers roll their cars so their front wheels are touching a light beam that crosses the start line. This is called staging the cars. Once the cars are staged, the starting official activates the Christmas Tree lights.

The front wheels of the dragsters have to line up at their starting point exactly before the race can begin.

ivers first see three amber-colored
hts. Fractions of a second later, a
een light flashes and the drivers hit
e gas and roar down the track! But
they leave the starting line too soon, they
e disqualified. They also have to remain
tirely inside their own racing lane.

ag racers look for two measurements
ter a race: time and speed. The elapsed
ne measures how long it takes them to
ver the quarter-mile (0.4 km). Speed
measured at its highest point near the
ish. The winner of a race is the one
th the lowest elapsed time. Because
ey may have been slightly faster to start
e race, a driver with a lower speed may
st a faster elapsed time. Successful
ag racers must be great drivers, but they
so must have super-fast reactions to the
nking Christmas Tree.

Racers watch this Christmas Tree to start a race. After the amber-colored lights flash, the green blinks and the drivers hit the gas!

INSIDE STORY ||||||||

Keep It Fair

Race officials can inspect the cars and
engines before and after each NHRA drag
race. Teams have to follow a strict set of
rules on what materials are used to make
their cars. Sometimes a team tries to shave
off tenths of a second or gain a little speed
by breaking these rules. If this happens,
their car and team can be fined by NHRA
or even disqualified. But DQs, which mean
disqualified, like these are rare. No one
wants to win, and then lose!

GO FAST, THEN STOP!

Going fast is one thing, but how do the cars stop?

Drag racers reach speeds above 300 miles per hour (480km/h)—and then they have to stop! The brakes work to stop the cars when they are going that fast. Special heavy-duty brakes press against the inside of the fast-spinning wheels and begin to slow the car down.

Just as drivers reach the finish line, they use another stopping device—a parachute! Pushing a button in the car pops out a large parachute from the back of the car.

The parachutes pop out of special boxes at the back of the dragsters.

Stretching out on very strong cables called shrouds, the large silk parachute expands almost instantly to catch the air and slow down the car. Special boxes in the back of the cars hold the parachutes. They are connected to the drivers by cables. Race teams take great care in packing these parachutes. They have very special ways of folding them so they come out smoothly and without tangling. A car that has a parachute failure can get in serious trouble. Several bad wrecks have resulted from broken parachutes.

The huge parachutes don't stop the car completely, but they help it slow down quickly.

BIG SLICKS: DRAGSTER TIRES

Dragster tires are literally where the rubber meets the road.

Drag racers use very special tires designed for their unique type of racing. Most dragster tires are much bigger than the tires of a family car. The rear wheels used in Top Fuel can be nearly 4 feet (1.2 m) tall and almost 10 feet (3 m) around. Compare that to a passenger car, which has tires that are 2–3 feet (0.6–0.9 m) tall. Dragster tires are about 17 inches (43 centimeters) across.

Drivers do a burnout to help heat the rubber and create a better grip on the track.

Here's a good look at the wide, smooth tires on this Funny Car.

Also, unlike most tires, dragster tires are smooth. They do not have **treads**, or grooves, cut into their surface. Because of this, dragster tires are called slicks. The smooth surface lets the tire grip the road more tightly.

Dragster tires are also somewhat softer than your average car tires because they move at such hot, high speeds that they need to expand without blowing. The softer rubber makes this possible. Some dragster tires have grooves on the side to help them expand safely when heated, too. As the tire grows in size, the grooves spread out.

Race teams must have lots of tires on hand at a race. With all the runs, burnouts, and soft tires, they may go through a dozen sets of rear tires in a day.

■ INSIDE STORY ||||||

Burnouts

Moments before the start of Top Fuel and Funny Car races, huge clouds of smoke rise from the back of the cars. Are the engines on fire? No, it's just time to burn out. Using the brake and **accelerator**, drivers spin their tires very fast on the hard asphalt surface without letting the car move forward. The spinning heats up the rubber of the tires, which helps them get a good grip on the road. Without this grip, the car would not be as quick off the starting line, or as fast down the track. Also, drivers often have water put on the tires before a burnout to help clean them.

FAMOUS TRACKS

For drag racing fans, some tracks are as famous as the drivers.

The NHRA holds its races on more than twenty drag strips located around the country. Here's a look at three of the most well-known and historic strips.

Since 1961 the most famous drag strip in the United States has been in Pomona, California, east of Los Angeles, a strip now known as the Auto Club Raceway. (A car owners' organization pays a fee to the track to use its name.) Pomona is also the site of the annual NHRA Finals. They have been held there since 1984. The track was built to take dangerous, illegal drag racing off the streets. In fact, the Pomona Police Department helped raise the money to build the track!

Race officials and fans who paid big money sit in the building behind the starting line at the drag race track in Pomona, California.

On the East Coast, the most famous drag strip is in Englishtown, New Jersey. Raceway Park opened there in 1965. Englishtown's biggest race each summer is the Supernationals.

The city of Indianapolis is also no stranger to motor sports. The famous Indy 500 has been held there since 1911. About 7 miles (11.3 km) from the Indianapolis Motor Speedway is O'Reilly Raceway Park, named after its sponsor, O'Reilly Auto Parts. The Indianapolis strip, which opened in 1958, has been the home of the NHRA U.S. Nationals races since 1961. The facility is also home to a 2.5-mile (4-km) auto-racing track.

The largest drag race track on the East Coast is in Englishtown, New Jersey. Fans there await the start of this Top Fuel race.

INSIDE STORY |||||||

The Lions Legend

Smaller drag strips were built around the country in the 1940s and 1950s. From 1955 to 1972 the most famous local strip was the Lions Drag Strip in Wilmington, California, near Long Beach. The first day the strip opened, more than ten thousand people showed up—organizers had expected a few hundred. The drag racing craze just kept going for two decades, as the top drivers in the sport, pro and amateur, headed to Lions to strut their stuff. It was still going strong when neighborhood groups banded together to close the strip. Drag racing fans were stunned, but still look back at that dusty strip with fond memories.

Drag racing fans circle some big events on their calendars every year, looking for big thrills and memorable moments.

The NHRA holds nearly two dozen race weekends every year, with champions crowned each weekend. In a way this is unique to drag racing. All of the names of the events include the word *Nationals*, which separates these races from local races held in the same places at other times during the year. Here's a look at some of the key events on the annual NHRA schedule.

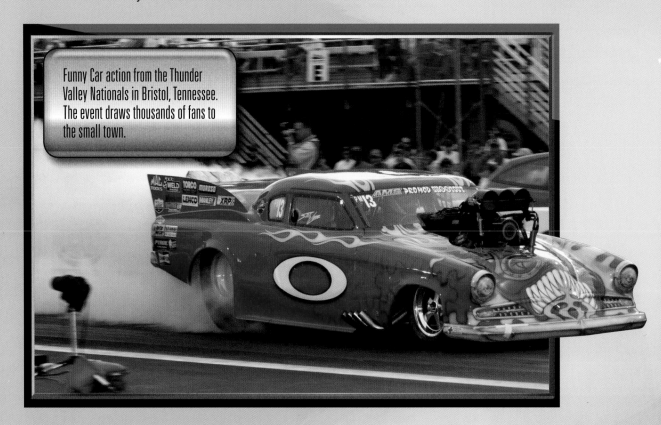

Funny Car action from the Thunder Valley Nationals in Bristol, Tennessee. The event draws thousands of fans to the small town.

Every year the season starts with the Winternationals, which is always held at Pomona, California. For many fans, this is their version of the green light. The February event breaks the off-season time-out, which has lasted since the previous November. For more than forty years, no driver managed to win this event in two consecutive years until Larry Dixon did so in 2002 and 2003.

Night racing is made more spectacular by the flaming exhaust from this Top Fuel dragster. This action is from the U.S. Nationals, held every year in Indianapolis, a national hotbed of auto racing in many forms.

Bristol, Tennessee, is the home of the Thunder Valley Nationals, a spring stop for the NHRA. Race fans turn this small town into a festival of speed.

In June, drivers head east to Englishtown, New Jersey. The Supernationals at Raceway Park have always featured amazing competitions.

The U.S. Nationals are one of the oldest drag racing competitions. They've been held every year since 1954. Since 1961 their home has been in Indianapolis. These races have witnessed some of the biggest wins in the sport's history.

The season wraps up back where it started, in Pomona. In recent years the races on these nail-biting final days have been dramatic. For instance, in 2006 and 2007, Tony Schumacher needed to win the final race of the day to clinch a season championship—and he won both times!

■ INSIDE STORY ||||||

Name Change

Major races in motor sports are usually named after a company that pays to sponsor the race. The company or its product name is mentioned hundreds of times as the race is discussed and promoted. But that can be confusing because sponsors can change from year to year. A race might be the O'Reilly Supernationals one year and the AC Delco Supernationals another. To keep it all straight, race fans should compare locations from year to year, instead of names. That way, you can look at what Don Garlits did at Englishtown versus what Tony Schumacher did there, instead of trying to match the race names, which were different.

A DAY AT THE RACES

A trip to a drag strip is a giant thrill—and a loud one— for racing fans of all ages.

Drag racing fans know that there is one thing they can't afford to leave at home: ear plugs! The enormous engines used by drag racers produce tremendous noise when revving up and accelerating. Fans know to bring earplugs, headsets, or earmuffs of some sort. Fans often also bring binoculars to watch the action on the track.

These two cars head to the starting line to be set up for a race.

The seating for a drag race is along one or both sides of the track. There are also pit areas, known as the **pits**, behind or at one end of the stands where race teams work on the cars. You can choose to sit near the starting line, with its huge burnouts, Christmas Tree, and busy activity, or further down the track to watch the cars roar by at high speed. You can also park yourself at the finish line to see the winners flash across in triumph.

Visit the Pits

One of the cool things about NHRA races is that fans can visit the pit areas. You can get up-close looks at the engines, paint schemes, and giant tires on these cars. You can ask questions (be polite for best results!) and even get autographs from some of the top drivers. Drag racers are very friendly, and they enjoy sharing their love of cars with their fans!

Announcers whip the crowd into excitement with details about the cars and racers as the cars are staged. Post-race announcements fill everyone in on time and speed. Giant video boards at some tracks also give you replays of the action and other details.

Though drag fans long for a big NHRA National, there are thousands of smaller drag races across the country at local strips. If you can't make it to Pomona, Indy, or Englishtown, some of the big stops on the NHRA tour—hit the local track and cheer for your friends and neighbors!

Big Daddy, Smokin' Joe, and Cha-Cha: No, not a list of boxers' names, but some of the finest Top Fuel drag racers of all time.

Don "Big Daddy" Garlits could be the "king of the dragsters." Beginning in 1955 with his first big win, he put together a legendary career at the Top Fuel level. No one has won more than Big Daddy's 144 races.

Garlits won the U.S. Nationals eight times, more than any other driver, and was a nine-time Top Fuel driver of the year. He was the first driver in Top Fuel to top just about every major speed landmark from 170 miles per hour (275 km/h) to 270 miles per hour (435 km/h).

Unlike most drivers, who just work behind the wheel, Garlits built his own cars, calling them all Swamp Rat and numbering them. By the time his career ended, he had reached all the way up to No. 34.

Here's "Big Daddy" Don Garlits in the cockpit of his Top Fuel dragster. Like all his cars, it was called The Swamp Rat. Heavy metal bars around him are known as the roll cage.

Garlits has won just about every award in the sport. In 2001 he became the top drag racer of all time. In 2002, to prove that Big Daddy still had his driving chops, he took one of his Swamp Rat cars out of his museum in Florida and roared it to a career-best 323.04 miles per hour (520 km/h)!

"Smokin'" Joe Amato took his childhood love of cars to the highest point of the Top Fuel world. From 1982–2000 he finished in the top ten every year. In an all-time record, for five of those years he was the NHRA champion, including three in a row from 1990–1992. Amato was the first driver to include a high rear wing on his vehicle, an innovation that all drivers quickly copied.

Another drag racing hero proudly drove a pink car. Shirley "Cha-Cha" Muldowney was a three-time Top Fuel champion, making her the most successful female motor sports athlete of all time. Her win in 1977 made her a national name and a hero to women everywhere. Cha-Cha won again in 1980 and 1982. She came a long way from having to battle race organizers in the 1960s who didn't think women should be racing.

Muldowney always painted her drag racing machines bright pink, to show she was proud of being a pioneer.

■ INSIDE STORY ▌▌▌▌▌▌

Scott Kalitta

One of the hard parts of drag racing is the danger its drivers face. The cars protect them as much as possible, but when a bad crash happens, it can be a disaster. Such a wreck ended the life of a great Top Fuel champion in 2006. Scott Kalitta was the 1994 Top Fuel champion, and the son of Connie Kalitta, a top driver in the 1960s. Wrecks are not as common as they once were since safety standards are much higher today . . . but accidents do happen. Kalitta's tragic death shows what a risk the drivers take to go fast . . . and to win.

Nothing funny about how good Don Prudhomme and Kenny Bernstein were—they're two of the best Funny Car drivers ever.

Though John Force has since overtaken their records, Prudhomme and Bernstein were the first real national stars in the Funny Car competition.

Kenny Bernstein started in Funny Cars but became one of the fastest Top Fuel drivers of all time.

Prudhomme "The Snake" dominated the class in the mid–1970s, winning four straight titles from 1975–1978. He got his nickname for being so quick off the starting line. In 1975 and 1976 Prudhomme dominated, winning thirteen out of sixteen events, and by the early 1980s, was the first Funny Car driver to cover the quarter-mile (0.4 km) in less than 6 seconds. His battles with Tom "The Mongoose" McEwen helped the sports world pay attention to the then-young sport of NHRA drag racing. Even today Prudhomme is an important team owner, helping Top Fuel Larry Dixon capture a pair of NHRA titles.

■ INSIDE STORY ▐▐▐▐▐▐▐

Dave Schultz

This Pro Stock Motorcycle superstar, who passed away from cancer in 2001, remains an example for all future motorcycle drag racers. Dave won six NHRA season titles, more than any other driver, and his forty-five race wins are the most ever. He was so consistent, he finished in the top five in the points standings for fourteen straight seasons. His 1994 season is a good example of his dominance: He won nine of the eleven races, including a record eight in a row.

In 1985 Kenny Bernstein won his first title in Funny Car racing, and four years later, he had matched "The Snake" Prudhomme's quartet of championships. Bernstein became a multitalented superstar, as he later went on to become the first driver to add a Top Fuel title to his Funny Car championships.

In 1992 Bernstein made driving history by becoming the first person ever to top 300 miles per hour (480 km/h) in a quarter-mile (0.4 km) race. One expert called it the biggest achievement in NHRA history.

Though Pro Stock doesn't get as much national attention, it isn't because of lack of help from Bob Glidden. No other driver has won as many NHRA national titles in a class as Glidden's ten in Pro Stock. He won the first series title in 1974 and was still winning fifteen years later in 1989. Glidden's amazing record put him at No. 4 on the NHRA's all-time list of drivers.

Don Prudhomme was the fastest "Snake" on four wheels for decades. He won four NHRA Top Fuel championships.

DRAG STARS: TOP FUEL

If Tony Schumacher keeps it up, they might have to find another series for him to race in—he's just too good!

Schumacher was the Top Fuel champion every year from 2004–2008. He had another title back in 1999, giving him five overall and tying him with legend Joe Amato for most Top Fuel championships. Schumacher won his 2006 and 2007 titles in style, coming through on the final pass of the last race of the season to clinch the top spots.

In 2004 he won ten races to set a single-season record for the series. His fifty-five race wins top all active drivers in Top Fuel.

How does Tony keep winning? Easy. He's very, very fast. In fact, he holds the Top Fuel speed record at 337.58 miles per hour (more than 540 km/h), set in 2005.

Tony Schumacher's car is sponsored by the U.S. Army.

Larry Dixon earned the NHRA Top Fuel national championship in 2002, and then again, in 2003.

Tony got his start in drag racing watching his dad. Don Schumacher was a top Funny Car driver in the 1960s. Tony's first season in Top Fuel was in 1997, and he became the overall champ only two years later. He remained among the top drivers for the next few seasons, though he had to come back from terrible wrecks twice. Tony just loves making things move—his hobbies include riding Harley-Davidson motorcycles.

Lots of drivers still challenge Tony. Larry Dixon was the Top Fuel champion in 2002 and 2003, and he's still among the leading drivers. His forty-two race wins are second only to Schumacher among active drivers. Antron Brown is among a handful of younger drivers aiming to knock Schumacher off his perch. Brown is a former Pro Stock motorcycle rider who moved to Top Fuel in 2008.

■ INSIDE STORY ||||||

Lady at the Wheel

The driver pushing Schumacher the hardest during the 2008 season was fast, talented, and determined. She was also one of a small group of women excelling at the highest level of motor sports. Hillary Will worked her way up through the ranks of lower racing classes to reach Top Fuel in 2006. By 2008 she was among the best, winning a big race in Indiana that pushed her into second place overall, behind Schumacher. As a former college gymnast and swimmer, she quickly showed that she could keep the pace with the big guys.

DRAG STARS: FUNNY CARS

When talking about Funny Cars, there's only one name to know: Force . . . John Force.

The veteran driver has won an amazing fourteen NHRA Funny Car championships. After winning every title in the 1990s, except in 1992, he kept going fast in the 2000s. His championship in 2006 showed that "The Force" was still with Funny Cars. Force also survived a terrible accident in 2007 that left him with numerous broken bones.

Force got his start in Funny Car racing in 1979, but it was only in 1990 that he won his first title. He made up for lost time quickly, dominating the decade. Among the highlights were breaking Don Prudhomme's record for career wins. He has since put it pretty much out of reach with a total of 126 wins through 2008. In 1996 he won thirteen races and was named the motor sports Driver of the Year. He is the only drag racer ever to win that honor.

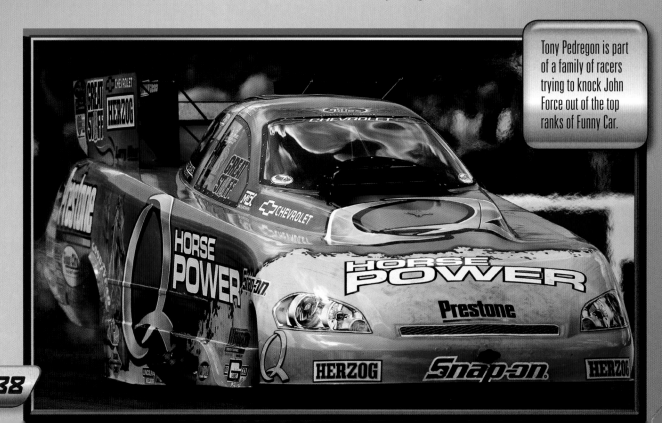

Tony Pedregon is part of a family of racers trying to knock John Force out of the top ranks of Funny Car.

John Force is just that in drag racing— a force. He dominated Funny Car racing for more than a decade.

Normally, the title goes to a NASCAR or Formula 1 driver. On the all-time NHRA list of top drivers, Force trails only legend Don "Big Daddy" Garlits.

Force is such a big star on the Funny Car circuit that it takes a family to beat him. Cruz and Tony Pedregon combined have sixty-seven wins. Each of them has also won a season championship: Cruz in 1992 and Tony in 2003. Both are still active in the division; Cruz was again at the top of the rankings in 2008. They're following in the tire tracks of their father, Frank, who was a Top Fuel driver in the 1960s. Tony is also a fine artist. He decorated his and his brother's helmet, as well as those of other drivers.

■ INSIDE STORY ▌▌▌▌▌▌

Awesome Ashley

Talk about a fast start—Ashley Force learned how to drive from the best, her dad John, the all-time Funny Car champ. She started driving in 2002 and got her Funny Car license in 2006. During her first season on the NHRA circuit, she and her dad were the subjects of a reality TV show. She gave the TV crew something good to film, finishing in the top ten in the points standings and earning Rookie-of-the-Year honors.

Jack Beckman is another top Funny Car driver. He's younger than Force and the Pedregons, but he's just as fast. He started out in Top Fuel and switched to Funny Cars in 2006. He's been near the top of the rankings ever since. Beckman is used to going fast, but only in the sky—he used to be in the Air Force.

DRAG STARS: PRO STOCK

For a decade, the name to watch in Pro Stock has been Jeg Coughlin Jr.

Jeg Coughlin Jr. got off to a fast start in drag racing. He was the 1998 NHRA Rookie of the Year and finished second in the points standings in 1999. By 2000 he was the Pro Stock champ. He won again in 2002. Coughlin won it all again in 2007 and 2008 as well. Jeg's fifty-three race wins are among the most of all time. Family dinnertime must be fast—Jeg is one of four brothers who are all race car drivers.

When Jeg didn't win, Greg Anderson did. He won the Pro Stock titles in 2003, 2004, and 2005. During the 2003 win, he set a series record with twelve race wins.

Three-time Pro Stock champion Greg Anderson took advantage of Jeg Coughlin's year off to win the 2003 title.

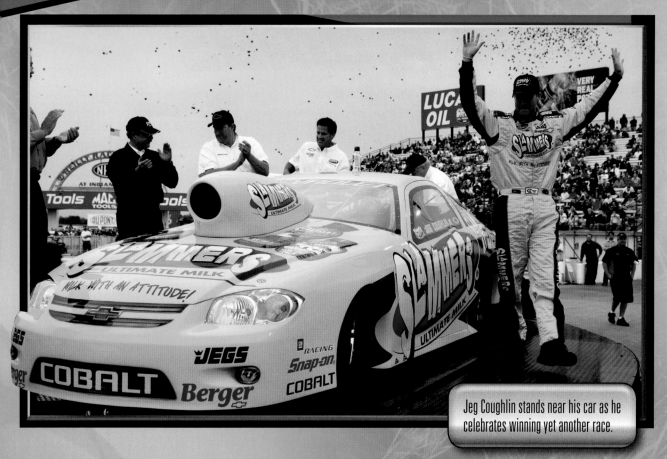

Jeg Coughlin stands near his car as he celebrates winning yet another race.

In fact, Greg outnumbers Jeg with fifty-six wins. Greg has been really consistent, finishing among the top three in final season points standings every year since 2003.

Jason Line is another former champion looking to return to the top. He won the 2006 overall title. The next year he set a national Pro Stock speed record at 211.69 miles per hour (340.68 km/h).

Kurt Johnson is still looking for his first season title, but he can boast one remarkable streak: He has won at least one race a year for thirteen consecutive seasons. Kurt was the 1993 Rookie of the Year and has been in the top ten every year since, a remarkable run of success.

■ INSIDE STORY ||||||

The Veteran

Both Anderson and Coughlin have a long way to go to catch up to Warren Johnson. The six-time champ (1992, 1993, 1995, 1998, 1999, and 2001) is still out there, racing and winning. Overall, his ninety-six race wins are the most ever in Pro Stock, while his six season titles are second only to legendary Bob Glidden's seven. Warren got his start way back in 1982 and his list of Pro Stock firsts is as long as the drag strip. He was the first to top 180, 190, and 200 miles per hour (290, 305, and 320 km/h). He might be old enough to be the father of many a driver, but he can still beat many of them off the line.

OTHER WAYS TO DRAG

Drag racing doesn't stop at the top, with Top Fuel, Funny Car, and Pro Stock classes.

The NHRA features twelve classes of racing, including more than two hundred types of vehicles. The difference between some of them may be slight to outsiders, but they mean a world of difference to drag racers.

Just below the top three automobile drag levels are the Top Alcohol Dragster and Funny Car divisions. These cars are similar to those at the top level, but run on methanol, a different type of fuel. Their **transmission** is also slightly different, but the body types are almost the same as the top levels. Each can run about 10 to 15 percent slower than the big boys.

Top Alcohol dragsters look like Top Fuel cars, but run on different fuel.

This Stock dragster is based on the popular Chevrolet Camaro.

In Comp Class competitions, you have to be good at math. By using a formula that compares the weight of a car to the size of its engine, race officials create an index number for each car. Cars are then matched according to their numbers. This means that the race will come down to a driver's skill instead of engine power.

The Stock category uses cars that are most like those you see on the street. One of the rules of the division is that the cars be nearly the same as the cars that come out of the factories, though teams can add racing slicks and a few smaller engine parts. Drivers compete in a wide range of cars in this category.

If you like to drive fast, you can find a way to do it, legally and safely. See you at the finish line!

■ INSIDE STORY ▐▐▐▐▐▐▐

Drag Racing on TV

You can watch the NHRA's top races on national cable sports channels. You can also watch the drag racing TV show called *Pinks*, which is often seen on the Speed Channel. The title comes from the nickname of a car's registration papers. The show matches up cars of a similar size and speed, and winners literally take the car from the loser! Drivers are more often the kind of people you see everyday instead of professionals. The action is fast, furious, and fun!

DRAG RACING CHAMPIONS

TOP FUEL

Year	Champion
1974	Gary Beck
1975	Don Garlits
1976	Richard Tharp
1977	Shirley Muldowney
1978	Kelly Brown
1979	Rob Bruins
1980	Shirley Muldowney
1981	Jeb Allen
1982	Shirley Muldowney
1983	Gary Beck
1984	Joe Amato
1985	Don Garlits
1986	Don Garlits
1987	Dick LaHaie
1988	Joe Amato
1989	Gary Ormsby
1990	Joe Amato
1991	Joe Amato
1992	Joe Amato
1993	Eddie Hill
1994	Scott Kalitta
1995	Scott Kalitta
1996	Kenny Bernstein
1997	Gary Scelzi
1998	Gary Scelzi
1999	Tony Schumacher
2000	Gary Scelzi
2001	Kenny Bernstein
2002	Larry Dixon
2003	Larry Dixon
2004	Tony Schumacher
2005	Tony Schumacher
2006	Tony Schumacher
2007	Tony Schumacher
2008	Tony Schumacher

FUNNY CAR

Year	Champion
1974	Shirl Greer
1975	Don Prudhomme
1976	Don Prudhomme
1977	Don Prudhomme
1978	Don Prudhomme
1979	Raymond Beadle
1980	Raymond Beadle
1981	Raymond Beadle
1982	Frank Hawley
1983	Frank Hawley
1984	Mark Oswald
1985	Kenny Bernstein
1986	Kenny Bernstein
1987	Kenny Bernstein
1988	Kenny Bernstein
1989	Bruce Larson
1990	John Force
1991	John Force
1992	Cruz Pedregon
1993	John Force
1994	John Force
1995	John Force
1996	John Force

1997	John Force	1984	Lee Shepherd	
1998	John Force	1985	Bob Glidden	
1999	John Force	1986	Bob Glidden	
2000	John Force	1987	Bob Glidden	
2001	John Force	1988	Bob Glidden	
2002	John Force	1989	Bob Glidden	
2003	Tony Pedregon	1990	Darrell Alderman	
2004	John Force	1991	Darrell Alderman	
2005	Gary Scelzi	1992	Warren Johnson	
2006	John Force	1993	Warren Johnson	
2007	Tony Pedregon	1994	Darrell Alderman	
2008	Cruz Pedregon	1995	Warren Johnson	

PRO STOCK MOTORCYCLE

Year	Champion
1987	Dave Schultz
1988	Dave Schultz
1989	John Mafaro
1990	John Myers
1991	Dave Schultz
1992	John Myers
1993	Dave Schultz
1994	Dave Schultz
1995	John Myers
1996	Dave Schultz
1997	Matt Hines
1998	Matt Hines
1999	Matt Hines
2000	Angelle Sampey
2001	Angelle Sampey
2002	Angelle Sampey
2003	Geno Scali
2004	Andrew Hines
2005	Andrew Hines
2006	Andrew Hines
2007	Matt Smith
2008	Eddie Krawiec

PRO STOCK

Year	Champion
1974	Bob Glidden
1975	Bob Glidden
1976	Larry Lombardo
1977	Don Nicholson
1978	Bob Glidden
1979	Bob Glidden
1980	Bob Glidden
1981	Lee Shepherd
1982	Lee Shepherd
1983	Lee Shepherd

1996	Jim Yates
1997	Jim Yates
1998	Warren Johnson
1999	Warren Johnson
2000	Jeg Coughlin Jr.
2001	Warren Johnson
2002	Jeg Coughlin Jr.
2003	Greg Anderson
2004	Greg Anderson
2005	Greg Anderson
2006	Jason Line
2007	Jeg Coughlin Jr.
2008	Jeg Coughlin Jr.

GLOSSARY

accelerator   The gas pedal; the part of the car that a driver pushes to add gasoline to the engine to make the car move.

aerodynamics   The science of how air moves over objects.

dominant   The most successful or most powerful.

elapsed time   A measurement of how long it takes a drag racer to go from start to finish.

horsepower   A measurement that shows how much work an engine can do.

irregular   Different from what is normal.

methanol   An oil-based chemical used as fuel in drag racing.

nitromethane   Another oil-based chemical used as fuel in drag racing.

pits   The area at a race track where mechanics work on cars and engines.

traction   The grip that a moving object has on a stationary one.

transmission   An assembly of parts of a car that include the speed-changing gears to help the engine move.

treads   The grooves on the outside of tires.

FIND OUT MORE

BOOKS

Von Finn, Danny. *Drag Racing* (Torque Books). Danbury, CT: Children's Press, 2008. More close-up pictures of drag racers, with a focus on the Top Fuel division.

Zuehlke, Jeffrey. *Drag Racers*. Minneapolis, MN: Lerner Books, 2007. Another basic look at drag racing, this book features awesome photos and background on top drivers.

WEBSITES

Visit these websites for more information:

www.draglist.com

This is a gathering of links and news posted by drag racing fans and experts. It's a good way to keep up on local drag racing events or find out technical information.

www.nhra.com

This is the official site of the NHRA. It is the best place to find out more about your favorite drivers, races, and cars. You can also read about how dragsters work and how drag racing got started.

INDEX